MW00779424

# Wet My Hands

## Dr. A.H. Yurvati

Copyright © 2021 Dr. A.H. Yurvati
All rights reserved
First Edition

Fulton Books
Meadville, PA

Published by Fulton Books 2021

ISBN 978-1-63985-788-3 (paperback)
ISBN 978-1-63985-789-0 (digital)

Printed in the United States of America

This book is dedicated to my lovely wife, Sharon. Without her guidance, encouragement, and love, I would not have had such a successful career. I also dedicate this to the friends, colleagues, residents, and students who I have had the pleasure of growing up with, working with, or teaching. If you identify yourself in my book, it's because you intersected with me in a special way. Finally, to all of my patients, who entrusted me to care for them at their most vulnerable time. I saved many, and some I could not. But I always gave my best.

# Acknowledgments

I want to thank Melissa Gannon, my artist, for doing a stellar job on the book jacket.

To Patrick and Sam at Medical City Fort Worth, who staged the photo Melissa utilized to create the graphics for *Wet My Hands*.

A very special acknowledgement to John Dykus, my editor, who took a piece of rubbish and transformed it into something worthy of my readers.

# Introduction

Life is a precious adventure that we are privileged to experience. But it comes with multiple variables, many beyond our control.

I was at the pinnacle of my career as a professor of surgery, a skilled surgeon, and a dedicated medical educator. Then I hurt my back lifting a riding mower onto a pickup bed. After three weeks of relentless back and leg pain, I acquiesced to an MRI. I suspected a ruptured disc. Wrong diagnosis, doctor! I had sustained a pathological fracture of my third lumbar vertebra, meaning cancer!

The Fates had snipped a portion of my life thread.

I underwent a five-and-a-half-hour spinal stabilization, and the biopsy proved cancer in the bone marrow—multiple myeloma. You can't cure this disease, only sequester it by chemotherapy, powerful doses of steroids, and perhaps a stem cell bone marrow transplant. I have experienced all of these indignities and more while, at the same time, trying to help my wife recover from a stroke.

Above all, you will find here a love story—one peppered with detours and achievements and lives saved, perseverance and triumphs, crushing diagnoses, and beat-the-odds rallies. It's three in the morning, I'm wide awake from the steroids, and I have much to tell you. Let's talk.

The ancient Greeks believed that the Fates control our days, that they assign individual destinies to mortals at birth. They spin, weave, and cut the strings of life, much to their amusement. Even Zeus, the mightiest of the gods, feared the Fates—Clotho (Spinner), Lachesis (Allotter), and Atropos (Inflexible). I believe they have a tight grip on the hand brake and the throttle of my past, present, and future.

Welcome to my journey.

# Chapter 1

It was 1963, and I was attending a traditional Catholic school run by the "Sisters of No Mercy." I had trouble with math and scored poorly on exams. There I was, seven years old, standing in front of the class, my math paper emblazoned with a bright-red stamp. It was not an *A* (an angel with wings and a halo), *B* (angel, no halo), or *C* (angel, no halo or wings) but a *D* (the devil). Talk about playing Jedi mind games on an impressionable kid. This trauma stayed with me into my undergraduate studies when my lovely wife, Sharon, said, "You better get over this, or you'll never get into medical school." So I took a one-credit psychology course, Relieving Math Anxiety, at California State University. *Wham!* Numbers could never hurt me again.

Twelve years of Catholic school can mess you up. The nuns told me I would never amount to anything and that I might as well hang out on the street corner, smoking cigarettes. Allentown, Pennsylvania, has a lot of street corners. William Allen, one of eighteenth-century Pennsylvania's wealthiest men, founded Allentown in 1762. I grew up there. Interesting fact: During the American Revolutionary War, George Washington's army suffered defeat at the Battle of Brandywine; Philadelphia was defenseless, and Washington worried that the British would confiscate church bells in the area and melt them down to make cannons. He sent orders for the Pennsylvania State House Bell, now known as the Liberty Bell, and other bells to be transported north to Allentown. The Old Zion Reformed Church sheltered them under its wooden floors. The church still stands on Hamilton Street. The Liberty Bell Museum is on the building's lower level.

Allentown is an industrial city famous for Mack trucks. The Mack Brothers Co., founded in 1900, initially manufactured trolleys, buses, and hook-and-ladder fire trucks. During World War I, Mack delivered to the United States and British armies on the front lines around six thousand AC trucks. They functioned so well in the austere environment that the British started calling the AC a Mack bulldog. In 1932, while recuperating from surgery, Mack's chief engineer, Alfred Fellows Masury, carved a bulldog hood ornament out of a bar of soap (US Pat. 87931). The iconic bulldog has been associated with Mack trucks ever since. I actually have a Mack bulldog in my garage, and I saw one on eBay for $150. The last Mack truck rolled off the assembly line on October 24, 1987; and as the company moved production to Winnsboro, South Carolina, plant 5C (the place at which my dad seemed to be the happiest) was shuttered.

In Allentown, when you graduate high school, you might go off to college, but most went right to work either at Mack Trucks or at the neighboring Bethlehem Steel. I decided to get out of town and join the Army. I scored well on the entry examinations and was slotted to become an advanced army medic.

I was off to Fort Dix, New Jersey, for basic training. The drill sergeants thought they were tough, but they couldn't match the Sisters of No Mercy. Then came Fort Sam Houston in Texas and the next phase of my Army career: Basic Medic, called 91A. It was at Fort Sam that my life changed forever and for the better. I met Sharon.

And the Fates were just warming up.

# Chapter 2

I grew up on the north side of Allentown at 922 N Fifth Street. The row homes are still there, except they're called terrace homes, one next to the other with narrow, shared walls. Back then, they housed a mix of German, Pennsylvania Dutch, and English families. Six of us—my mom, dad, and four boys—lived in this three-floored row home with only one bathroom. I had the second-floor back bedroom and could listen to music and play the guitar. I had an old 1950s Zenith 2350RZ1 porthole black-and-white TV that came from my grandparents. It had a round twelve-inch screen, and it took fifteen minutes for the vacuum tubes to energize before you saw an image. I stayed up on the night of July 20, 1969, and witnessed Neil Armstrong exiting Apollo 11 and stepping on the moon. It was 8:17 UTC time, 8:17 p.m. in Allentown. It was an inspiring moment (I was fourteen) that lit a small fire in me that made me think, *Hey, I could do something fantastic with my life.*

I was a good student. I attended class, passed the tests, and moved along. I never really studied but somehow cleared each class one by one. I couldn't sit still and always liked to work, so I took a paper route. I delivered the newspaper twice a day. In the morning, I'd deliver the *Morning Call*, and in the evening, the *Evening Chronicle*. I became skilled at folding the papers to toss on the porches and accurate at landing them right at the center in front of the front door. I can still remember the headlines: "JFK Assassinated in Dallas," "Bobby Kennedy Assassinated," "Vietnam War Updates," "Moon Landing"—so much history.

I took a second job working for a lady at our corner grocery. Almost every neighborhood had a small grocery store and at least one beer joint. I helped her stock, then I waited on customers and learned how to use the dangerous meat slicer (excellent introduction to surgery). When she closed, I found another job at Fourth and Washington Streets in Ritter's Pharmacy.

Mr. Ritter was tall and lanky—a dead ringer for LBJ minus the Texas accent. He was the first mentor who saw my potential. I learned how to count pills and tablets, compound salves and creams, and, the trickiest of all, pour cough syrup from a one-gallon jug into a four-ounce narrow-neck bottle. Now that takes skill. I considered pharmacy school at the Philadelphia College of Pharmacy and Science but lacked both the grades and the money. Mr. Ritter sold the pharmacy to a younger pharmacist. But it wasn't the same, so I walked across the street to Eline's.

Eline's was a lot like Walgreens but without a pharmacy. I ran the soda fountain at the long lunch counter, made ice cream sundaes, and cooked cheesesteaks—an Allentown dietary requirement. After school, I'd walk home, go to the corner and hang out, and work the counter. (I first charmed Sharon with my famous marshmallow and peanut sundae in 1974, and I still make it for her.)

My first car was a 1964 Rambler American 440-H hardtop with a 3.2-liter I6 engine. Because the gasket seals were worn and the car had to park on the steep Fifth Street hill, it leaked oil so badly that I kept a case in the car and topped off the engine prior to starting. One of the neighbors, a German lady who constantly swept her porch, sidewalk, and gutter, would yell at me for leaking *feurzzeug*, "fire stuff" (meaning the oil), down her gutter. That car fostered many memories, including my first "twitter" (no, not social media) experiences.

Four blocks down the street at Ganci's garage, my friend Tommy and I learned how to tune, modify, and add carburetors to cars—you know, soup them up. I sold the Rambler and bought a 1964 Chevy Impala for cash at $250. We modified the engine, although the V block 283 and 327 were simple to work on. I added chrome wheels, jacked the suspension, and even spray-painted it a glistening metallic bronze. Now *that* was a Puerto Rican car! It was a great ride with lots of back-seat room for back-seat reconnaissance. Right after high school, I sold it to a classmate, and not two weeks later, it was stolen. It was found under a bridge, stripped. The PRs got it.

# Chapter 3

My father grew up in Allentown and lived on Maple Street. My grandfather was a glazier working for Pittsburgh Plate Glass. My grandmother was a homemaker. Years ago, my brother Bill, who loves genealogy, obtained an immigration record (no. 4701) for our great-grandmother on my father's side, born in Cerovo, Slovakia, on March 19, 1877. She was from an area in what was formerly central Europe encompassing the historical lands of Bohemia, Moravia, and Slovakia. Czechoslovakia was formed from several provinces of the collapsing Austria-Hungary empire in 1918 at the end of World War I. In the interwar period, it became the most prosperous and politically stable state in eastern Europe. The Nazis occupied it from 1938 to 1945, and it was under Soviet control from 1948 to 1989. On January 1, 1993, Czechoslovakia separated peacefully into two countries: the Czech Republic and Slovakia.

I went looking for the town. It took a while as immigration record no. 4701 has some interesting twists. First, our great-grandmother's name is spelled Yurovati versus the present Yurvati. Even today, some people call me Yurovati. Turns out Yurovati is correct. A few years after coming to America, my grandfathers, Paul and Albert, started feuding; and Albert dropped the O from his name. In the Sacred Heart of Jesus Catholic Cemetery in Whitehall, an Allentown suburb, numerous family plots are separated into the Yurovati section and the Yurvati section. The old feud survives on our headstones.

Then there's the spelling of the town in Slovakia where my grandmother lived. The clerk spelled it Cerove, but I could not find this village in any search engine. The correct spelling is Cerovo. Cerovo, Slovakia, was founded in 1273, the name deriving from the Hungarian word for *turkey oak*. A predominantly Lutheran community, it features the ruins of a castle, the Litava, and has tourism aspirations.

My great-grandmother Mary (maiden name Dashner) emigrated to the United States on the SS *Kaiser Wilhelm III*, described as a third-class transport, entering New York on June 13, 1901. She ended up in Allentown and married Stephen Yurovati on June 7, 1903. She gave birth to seven children: Mary, Rose, Albert, Margaret, Francis, William Joseph, and Paul. Stephen died on July 25, 1934. I am the third Albert, named after my father and grandfather—not much creativity there. Sharon says that if you look at the Yurvati family crest, you'll find a war hammer with a broken handle held together with duct tape and the heading "Good Enough."

My father attended the same school as I, Central Catholic, and was an honors student. He was quiet, reserved, and nonconfrontational, and he loved pulling trout from the Lehigh River and Little Lehigh Creek in Allentown. He had the grades for college but no money, so he joined the Marines and had his basic training at Camp Lejeune in North Carolina. (In March 2010, the month of my cancer diagnosis, one Paul Buckley of Hanover, Massachusetts, received a 100 percent service-related disability from the Department of Veterans Affairs linking his cancer, multiple myeloma, to contaminated drinking water laced with strontium-90. The dreaded Fates!)

After basic training, my father was shipped off to Korea with an infantry unit, which caused him much anguish as the recruiters had promised him a quartermaster position. During this time, certain cerebral biochemical imbalances began to emerge. My brother Bill found in our father's Marine medical records that when he feigned a suicide attempt with aspirin, he was examined and deemed "not a psychiatry risk" and fit for duty. One year after deployment, he returned to the United States and was assigned to Vieques, Puerto Rico, an island municipality eight miles east of the main island.

On the eastern end of "Little Girl Island" (*Isla Nena*) was Camp Garcia, named after Pvt. First Class Fernando Garcia, a Medal of Honor recipient who fought in Korea and was a native Puerto Rican. It was on this tiny island (twenty miles by eight miles) that my father met and fell in love with my mother, Ivelise. (Growing up, I had a hard time explaining her name to kids whose mothers had more common names; Ivelise is of Puerto Rican origin and means "beautiful.") Albert and Ivelise married in the small *iglesia Catolica* in the Muñoz Rivera Plaza, the centerpiece of Isabel Segunda on the north side of the island. My father was discharged from the Marines and headed home to Allentown with his Puerto Rican bride. My brothers think she mistakenly believed she hit the lottery and married a rich American.

This story has yet another angle. When my mother was very young, she became pregnant by an older man on the island. She left my half brother, Jorge, with our grandmother, who raised him as her own.

So my parents arrived in Allentown, and my mom spoke little English and was so afraid of people that she sequestered herself in their small apartment on Brook Street. My dad worked at Mack Trucks, plant 4B, assembling vehicles one bolt at a time. I guess the repetitive tasks kept him happy. He later moved to plant 5C, where he masked the cabs for painting—very precise work. It likely gave him solace.

After work, my dad would gather up my mom and go patrol the riverbanks while she stayed in the car. He caught some major trophy fish over the years, including two preserved beauties hanging on my garage wall. On March 29, 1955, just before the opening of trout season, he was out "studying the fish." My mom was in the car, scared of the dark, when suddenly a scream in Spanish pierced the night. My dad dashed from the bushes to see an Allentown police officer holding a flashlight over a scared Puerto Rican woman. The officer thought some teens were making out in the car. Instead, it was my mother going into labor. The Fates extruded my life threads and wove them, and out I came.

A year or so later, the Yurovatis moved to 922 N Fifth Street, where my mom would produce three more boys: Bill, Bob, and Matt. We spent a lot of time outside as we had a back yard and Jordan Park was right down the street. The outside activity helped us burn off extra testosterone.

We were like wrecking balls out of control. Back then, you controlled such behavior with the dreaded strap; today, the authorities would take your kids and arrest you for felony injury to a child.

On Sundays, we'd pack into the car for a drive, parents in the front with the youngest, Matt, and the rest of us crammed in the back seat with no seatbelts. We especially enjoyed the Lehigh Valley Parkway, a lovely meander along the Lehigh River. High traffic kept the excursion under an hour; my dad incessantly complained about too many cars. Those rides were the extent of any family vacation other than going to Dorney Park. Solomon Dorney owned the land on which the park was built. It opened in 1884, and the entrance had a large clown, Alfundo, juggling balls (the name Alfundo being a combination of the words *Allentown*, *fun*, and *Dorney*). The park is famous for the Thunderhawk roller coaster built by Philadelphia Toboggan Coasters. Debuted in 1932, it remains the oldest continuously operating wooden roller coaster in the world.

Other than Dorney Park, we never ventured beyond Allentown. My father was plagued with a severe mental illness and had a very narrow comfort zone for new experiences. He was labeled a paranoid schizophrenic. Now the diagnosis would be bipolar schizoaffective disorder, an exceptionally rare (only 0.3 percent) type of mental illness characterized by traits of both schizophrenia and bipolar mood disorder. Men exhibit the disorder early in life, and my dad showed textbook characteristics. Medications helped if he took them, which he did until he felt better, then he stopped. He spent time at the Allentown State Hospital on Hanover Street. The facility was built in 1901 and closed on December 17, 2010.

He underwent inpatient psychiatric care and electroconvulsive therapy, a crude procedure where transmitting 70–120 volts at eight hundred milliamperes to the brain induces seizures—a Draconian practice; it is akin to rebooting a computer. The Italian psychiatrist Ugo Corletti pioneered ECT (1938), and it works in about 50 percent of patients. But relapses within that 50 percent are common. My dad would enter the hospital, come out functional, worsen, and go back in. Amazingly, he held a full-time job, raised a family, and moved about in society. Few people outside the family or close neighbors knew our secret. Today, we can openly discuss mental illness, and treatment therapies have improved. I thank the Fates for not weaving the psychiatric disorder thread into my life tapestry.

# Chapter 4

Since I had the second-floor back bedroom, that put Matt in the second-floor small bedroom by the bathroom; Bob and Bill had the third-floor upstairs bedrooms. We did not have air conditioning, and Allentown summers can be brutal. The third floor was an oven. But we all had our own spaces to escape the stress of our father's mental issues.

David Olmstead designed the radiant heater in 1834. It's a sealed, hollow cast-iron container with fins through which steam flows, and the fins get extremely hot. Steam pipes and radiators are prone to banging sounds similar to that of a steam hammer, created when some of the steam condenses in a horizontal section of the piping. The steam picks up the water, forms a "slug," and hurls it into a pipe fitting, making a loud noise and greatly stressing the pipe. Poor drainage often caused by buildings settling and the condensate pooling in pipes and radiators prevents the water from making its way back toward the boiler. This usually occurred deep in the night and scared the heck out of us kids.

In the fall, Sacred Heart Church would designate a day for visitations—first, the nuns, then the priests. So it was a Friday night, and we all were told to be home, bathe, and look respectable as the nuns were coming. The doorbell rang, and I went to answer and just about died on the spot. There on the front porch were two Fates disguised as nuns!

Sr. Judith Marie and Sr. Mary Agnes came in and sat down in our living room. My dad was drinking a beer and offered them a bottle.

"Sure," they said.

He asked, "Neuweiler or Horlacher?"

Neuweiler was the third-oldest brewery in Allentown, founded in 1911 (closed in 1968). Horlacher was the second oldest, founded in 1866 and closed in 1978. My dad bought beer by the case, so there was plenty. A few hours later, it was getting spirited, and the "Fates" told my mom that I was a good student but would never amount to anything. They suggested that perhaps the priesthood would be a good fit. But I was into girls! I was ruined. Thank goodness the lousy Fates did not weave that cord into my life tapestry.

My mom herded all the boys into the kitchen and gave us a stern warning: "Do not let anyone know your dad got the nuns drunk." We all went back to the living room, and suddenly my mom called out in Spanish, "*Ay, Dios mios!*" We had a statue of the Sacred Heart, and there was Jesus with his left hand pointing to the heart and his right hand raised as if giving a blessing. On closer inspection, someone had rolled a joint and placed it between his fingers. Needless to say, after the nuns left, out came the strap.

About a month later, one of the priests came to visit; it was subdued in the kitchen as my dad was going into one his depressions. Soon, my dad went back to Allentown State Hospital for more ECT. Becoming a priest was out of the question as I was going to hell anyway.

I was serving as an altar boy for the monsignor's 6:00 a.m. Mass. Half asleep, I tripped on my cassock, and his chalice with the Holy Communion went flying across the vestibule with a clang. I bent the crap out of his chalice, and the communion went everywhere. Uh-oh, the Fates. I am going to hell for sure!

Our house had a basement, which we called the cellar. It was basically the hewn-out bedrock that the house sat on. It was unfinished, but my father and grandfather poured a rough floor and whitewashed the walls. It was spooky, cold, and damp, and you'd get a chill going down there at night. All the homes used coal furnaces, which had a chute on the front of the house below the porch. The truck would come and dump anthracite (hard coal) into the coal bin. Anthracite is found only in Pennsylvania and burns the hottest of all fossil fuels at 25 million Btu—ideal for heating a three-story home. When my dad converted to oil heating, the attached coal bin became the perfect place for raising worms. He built wooden containers then filled them with dirt and earthworms. They were huge fat, slimy things—an ideal snack for unsuspecting brown trout.

One day, we found in the basement a Big-Bang Cannon. A physics assistant professor at Lehigh University in Allentown patented his "gas gun" in 1907 as an alternative to injury-causing fireworks. Pouring dry calcium carbide into a chamber containing a little water made acetylene gas. Push a button on the spark-coil igniter, and the cannon would let off a loud bang with almost no recoil. The company touted acetylene as much safer than gunpowder. We would double-charge the cannon, and a bright flame would shoot out a few feet from the barrel. I challenge any grandpa today to let his boys play with an acetylene gas device.

My introduction to medicine came when I was five. Kids were rounded up over the summer of their fifth birthday for the obligatory tonsillectomy (I would not be admitted to a hospital again for fifty years). In 1960, ether anesthesia was still used as an inhalation agent for surgery. Diethyl ether, or simply ether, is an organic compound with the formula $(C_2H_5)_2O$, abbreviated as $Et_2O$. It is a by-product of the vapor-phase hydration of ethylene and is used to make ethanol. Ether was synthesized by Valerius in 1540, and a dentist, Crawford William Long, is credited with its first clinical use as a general anesthetic in 1846. However, ether is extremely flammable and may form an explosive vapor/air mixture, ignitable even by static electricity. I can still recall, clear as day, screaming as I was wheeled into the operating room and being held down as a drip mask was placed over my face. Suddenly I saw red bubbles and heard a loud buzzing. After a short time, I woke up and had the worst sore throat I have ever experienced. Post-op in the pediatric ward, I had lots of ice cream and Jell-O, my tonsils gone.

My grandparents, parents, uncles, and aunts all had dentures, and we all saw a Dr. Sipple, who was from Germany and had an office in his home on Hamilton Street. The office was dark and looming with a chair, instruments, a drill, and a porcelain spit bowl that constantly swirled water. The scariest collection of human skulls with teeth sat on a shelf facing the dentist chair. In keeping with family tradition, I have a mouth full of fillings. And I still dread going to the dentist.

# Chapter 5

My mom was a terrible cook, and my dad shied with vigor from trying fresh delicacies. We had the same menu every week. Monday was Dinty Moore Beef Stew, Tuesday was minute steak (overcooked to shoe-leather consistency), Wednesday was Spam, Thursday was baked chicken, Friday was fish (from the Lehigh River or Jordan Creek, probably contaminated due to the industrial waste), Saturday was cardboard pizza, and Sunday was Three Chefs cheesesteaks. You may ask, where were the fresh fruits and vegetables for growing boys? My dad thought all mushrooms were poisonous; it was not until I met Sharon did I know otherwise.

Holidays and birthday parties consisted of the same items: Charles chips and pretzels, Velveeta cheese, and the now-gone but previously famous Arbogast & Bastian ring bologna. The ring bologna came from a slaughterhouse down by the Lehigh River off Hamilton Street. A&B Meats was founded in 1887 and closed in 1984. In its heyday, it slaughtered four thousand hogs daily. Ring bologna (baloney) is a sausage derived from mortadella, and A&B's distinct flavor came from adding myrtle berries. We growing boys could eat a whole ring slathered with mustard. And we washed it down with soda from A-Treat Bottling Co. A-Treat is a local soda bottling company founded in 1918. It stopped production in 2015, but since the brand was purchased, production resumed. Our favorites were the cream, birch beer, and orange sodas.

Since our home was on the Fifth Street hill, winter sledding was supreme as the city would block Fifth Street off from Washington Street all the way past Greenleaf Street. My father complained because you couldn't park on the street. Occasionally, a car was parked at the curb, and a poor kid would lose control of his sled on that icy slope and face-plant into a tailpipe—my introduction to trauma and bleeding. So cool.

# Chapter 6

School was mind-numbing, one-way repetition. You went from elementary to middle school to high school. Middle school was in Sacred Heart in an old building across from our church and next door to the convent where the Sisters of No Mercy lived and no one ever entered. They wore the full habit—robe, bib, and head and face covering—and a large rope belt that I remember a cat o' nine tails hanging from, but I may not be accurate this many years later. It was in my formative years that the three Fates actually appeared on earth: Sr. Judith Marie, Sr. Mary Alice Claire, and Sr. Edward Beatrice. If anyone reading this book is someone who went to school with me, you will not be getting a good night's sleep tonight as they will be coming back to haunt you.

Sr. Judith Marie targeted me, and I never knew why. I had her for a teacher twice: first in fourth grade and again in eighth. Right now, I hold in my hand my original report cards, written in perfect cursive using fountain-pen ink. A former classmate who became the principal at Sacred Heart found them in a purge of old documents and sent them to me. I was marked down consistently on attentiveness and habits of home study. As an educator, you need to measure competencies; the nuns never saw me study or not study at home, so how did they know? I did poorly in arithmetic too and in handwriting (early doctor penmanship).

Sr. Mary Alice Claire was about four feet tall, round as a basketball, and had Popeye the Sailor arms that could whack you clear across a room. We boys often had to stay after class, sitting quietly at our desks with hands folded, as disciplinary action for being disruptive. A Puerto Rican guy named Ricardo, who was both smoking and shaving in the fourth grade, was not staying, so he opened the second-story window and was creeping along the ledge toward the next-door classroom. With scant concern for her safety, Sr. Mary Alice went out on the ledge, grabbed him, and, with one toss, threw him back inside. After he crashed into a few desks, she lit into him. We boys were speechless, and we folded our hands even tighter. We never saw Ricardo after that.

Grades 9 through 12 were next door in Central Catholic High School (CCHS), the top draw of all of the schools in the Allentown archdiocese. Our mascot was the Viking, and at sports events, one of our classmates enthusiastically played the part in a helmet and beard, carrying a short axe. CCHS introduced us to Sr. Edward Beatrice, aka Eddy Betty, for whom you could not do anything right no matter how hard you tried.

Around two months before graduation, a good friend got very ill, throwing up with severe right-lower-quadrant abdominal pain. You guessed it—acute appendicitis. He left class without permission and went to the pay phone to call his mother so she could take him to the dispensary, a precursor to the emergency room at the hospital across the street from the school. Eddy Betty came down the steps and smacked him on the head, and he got up and coldcocked her. She went flying down the hall as we boys watched in sheer terror. Holy Jesus, George, you hit a nun! Well, George survived and was being expelled from school. He was not allowed to graduate, but his father and uncle were contractors who did a lot of free work for the church. They went to the principal, looking like the Gambinos, and got George back in and allowed to graduate, and Eddy Betty went off to the retirement nunnery.

George became quite the entrepreneur. Plus, he's now a fantastic chiropractor and expert in spine rehab. He has been a tremendous help in my postsurgical recovery, talking me through core exercises from miles away. Anyway, George, even as a high school senior, was our beer distributor. Friday night was for a football or basketball game, but Saturday night was beer night at the Lehigh Parkway, a large public park along Little Lehigh Creek in Allentown and the most prominent park in the city. It follows the creek for three miles from the city center to Cedar Crest Boulevard. It is famous for

Bogert's Covered Bridge, built in 1841 and one of the oldest bridges in the United States.

On Fridays, George would collect the money for his beer run. Although, how could he buy alcohol with the legal age at the time being twenty-one? (We used to drive across the border to New Jersey where the legal age was eighteen, but that was a hassle.) George also supplied our principal with beer at a discount. On Saturday nights, we would all gather in the park, and George would open his trunk and pop the keg. We got raided by the Allentown police once. George grabbed the keg and ran through the woods. He couldn't risk losing his deposit for the keg and tap.

Besides beer, there were botanicals and pharmacological substances to meet and write poems about. One of our classmates, a genius, had access to weed (having cancer with bone pain, a little cannabis would be great, but it's still not legal in Texas). We called Tommy C. "the chemist." Somehow, he got hold of the formula for the synthesis of LSD (lysergic acid diethylamide): $C_{20}H_{25}N_3O$. LSD is naturally occurring, produced on the ergot fungus that grows on rye and other grains. The much-maligned Salem witches may have been young girls who ingested bread tainted with this fungus. The most famous person associated with LSD was Timothy Leary. He initially taught at Harvard in the department of psychology and was investigating the properties of hallucinogenic chemicals. Unfortunately, he liked to take the drugs with his subjects, so he was dismissed. He joined the faculty at the University of California–San Francisco and, in 1995, died of prostate cancer, but he used psychedelics into the last days of his life. Tommy C. synthesized the substance and dripped small dots on paper, which you put under your tongue. In a matter of minutes, you were tripping. It's a good day when you can actually see music.

One summer, we were parking late under the Albertus L. Meyers Bridge, which we called the Eighth Street Bridge. Meyers was the conductor of the Allentown Band and a coronet player with John Philip Sousa. The bridge is an open-span arch and, in 1913, was listed as the longest and highest concrete bridge in the world—2,650 feet end to end, 45 feet wide, and 138 feet tall, boasting nine arches. A young girl threw herself off the bridge, legend holds, and still haunts the place. There we were one night, and we saw her all in white with the most fearful look. We got the hell out, our hearts racing into ventricular tachycardia. We never went back to that spot. The ghost is real. We're sure. Or maybe it was the beers and the doobies.

We sometimes went to Yocco's, an Allentown hot dog/cheesesteak emporium founded in 1922 on Liberty Street. The true spelling is Iacocca, except the Pennsylvania Dutch could say *Yocco* more easily. Celebrated family member Lee Iacocca was instrumental at Ford Motor Co. in developing the Mustang; he became Ford's president but clashed with Henry Ford II and was fired. He eventually led Chrysler Corp. and orchestrated the 1979 federal bailout of the company.

Yocco's was in a small row home at a corner; it was not very wide and had a few tables and chairs. The Medford all-beef dogs came slathered in "secret sauce," mostly a spicy chili mixture, and I could eat six at a sitting in addition to an order of pierogies. I'm getting hungry just recalling the place. A world map on the wall had pins that showed all the places a Yocco's Doggie Pack had been shipped to. A ton of them went to Vietnam for the soldiers who were from Allentown. One night, we laced the weenies with just a hint of LSD. Now *that* was a hot dog.

I liked listening to music, so I went to the pawnshop, bought some big speakers, wired them into my record player, and fashioned a high-powered stereo. I liked Pink Floyd, the Who, and the Moody Blues. I still have my collection of Moody Blues vinyl. Listening to Super Lou on WAEB, I would open the bedroom window, light up a doobie, and dream of the future.

That future did not include college. I didn't have the money or the grades (academically ranked 227th out of 281 graduating seniors), and we were still at war in Vietnam. And my draft card number was 3(!)—a surefire statistical guarantee of being drafted. Enlisting seemed to be my only option. My ASVAB (Armed Services Vocational Aptitude Battery) scores were excellent, per the recruiter, and I was guaranteed an MOS (Military Occupation Specialty). I chose advanced 91C: Practical Nursing Specialist. The recruiter came to our house and met with my parents, and we signed papers allowing me to enlist. I was going in the Army.

# Chapter 7

High school graduation came along, and we headed to the Jersey shore where we rented a beach house for one last pharmaceutical and beer event. I left Allentown in June for Fort Dix, New Jersey, and basic training. I told friends that I was "going to find me a big-breasted blonde nurse from California." They all laughed, but I was mostly correct. She became a dietician.

I arrived at Fort Dix late in the evening. They fed us hot dogs and beans, and everyone was so nice welcoming us to the United States Army. I thought, *Wow, this ain't so bad,* and went off to my bunk, not realizing that during the night, the Fates would reweave one of my life threads. At 0500 hours, a screaming, raging drill sergeant was banging a bunk adapter on our racks, waking us all up for formation in our skivvies. Welcome to eight weeks of basic training.

We ran everywhere. We slogged through the sandy and some-times muddy trails. We trained with basic infantry, M16s, and hand grenades. We had a class on CBR (chemical, biological, radiological warfare) that required tearing with a gas mask. The "gas chamber" was an enclosed building in which the drill sergeants would activate a slow-burning pot of CS (crowd suppression) tear gas, also known as 2-chlorobenzylidene malononitrile. A German scientist created it in the late nineteenth century. The term *gas* is really a misnomer as the agent is composed of micropulverized powder that, when dispersed in the air, aerosolizes, resulting in uncontrollable tears, irri-tated breathing, and a feeling that your skin is burning.

We were instructed to take off our gas masks and recite our name, rank, serial number, and maybe home address until we had to take a breath. Our lungs were on fire, our eyes burned, and we wanted out of there. Actually, we were only in there maybe five minutes, but it seemed like a lifetime. Oh, I forgot to tell you that the day prior to our gas chamber training, we were all sent to the barber to get our heads shaved. Guess what CS does to raw skin!

We ate MREs (meals ready to eat) with chocolate bars in them that tasted like a wax candle. I learned from Sharon some food chemistry, and chocolate melts between eighty-six and ninety degrees Fahrenheit. The Army in 1937 commissioned Hershey Co. to develop a chocolate bar for field rations. Quartermaster Col. Paul Logan had four requirements: weigh four ounces, have considerable food energy (six hundred calories), be able to withstand high temperatures, and taste "a little better than a boiled potato" (to keep the soldiers from eating their emergency rations in nonemergency situations). The combination of fat and oat flour made for a brick, and the sugar did little to mask the bitterness of the dark chocolate. Since it was designed to hold up in heat, the bar was nearly impossible to bite into. Most men had to shave slices off before they could chew it. And thus, the Logan bar was created. The wrapper instructed that Field Ration D was to be eaten slowly over about half an hour, or it could be dissolved by crumbling into a cup of boiling water and consumed as a beverage.

Due to my scores on the Army's standardized tests, I was pulled out of my unit for a three-day SLPP (special leadership performance program) taught by a West Point lieutenant and an NCO. The latter, Drill Sergeant Whitley, was an imposing figure with two tours of duty in Vietnam. He had lost the distal portion of his ring finger, and he had deep scars on his lip and on the right side of his face, which were inflicted by a Claymore mine (to be precise, the M18A1). Its inventor, Norman McCloud, named it after a medieval Scottish sword. The mine is command detonated and directional and has a layer of C-4 explosives behind an epoxy resin embedded with seven hundred eight-inch steel balls. In seventy-two-point letters, it warns, "Front toward enemy." The mines were set on the perimeter, but during the night, the Viet Cong turned them toward the friendly. Badly hurt, Whitley was deployed out of the combat zone and ended up at Fort Dix, training recruits. I enjoyed this program. It was the first time in my life that I felt I could be someone people would follow and look up to. The Fates wove a heavy thread into my life fabric.

We graduated boot camp, and some in my company went to infantry training or other combat arms and then Vietnam. I still had two more programs to complete: Basic Medic, 91A, at Fort Sam in Houston, Texas, and Advanced Practical Nursing Training, 91B, at Fort Jackson in South Carolina. At graduation, I was promoted from private to private first class (PFC) and thought I was on my way to a twenty-year career. The Fates disagreed and rewove a thread of my life tapestry for the better.

# Chapter 8

There we were, active-duty Army soldiers and WACs, sitting in 91A basic medical class. The Army was integrating the Women's Army Corps into the regular army. The Women's Army Corps was founded in 1942 as the Women's Army Auxiliary Corps (WAAC) and was converted one year later to a branch of the US Army. The WAAC adopted Pallas Athena, Greek goddess of victory and womanly virtue, wise in peace and the arts of war, as its insignia. Athena was the daughter of Zeus, and she had no mother as she sprang from Zeus's head fully grown and clothed in golden armor. The WACs filled three major specialties. The brightest and nimblest were trained as switchboard operators. Next came the mechanics, who needed high equipment aptitude and problem-solving ability. The bakers were usually the lowest-scoring recruits and stereotyped as the least intelligent by their fellow WACs. The Women's Army Corps was disbanded in 1978. In 2015, Jeanne Price, the most tenured female warrant officer and last member of the Women's Army Corps, retired.

Sitting next to me was the most beautiful blonde I have ever seen—nice headlights and a radiant smile. The insignia on her lapel was the goddess Athena. Out of the corner of my eye, a hand flashed, and it tore my manual from my hands. This young lady was frustrated as she could not follow the instructions and wanted to read them for herself. Integrating women into the regular army was not going smoothly; there was a shortage of manuals, and the guys got them first.

I was smitten by Athena, the Greek goddess of war, the symbol of the Women's Army Corps, and Sharon's incarnate goddess. My blood was on fire.

The men had the unusual nighttime barracks fire watch, but in addition, we had post patrol. We walked six square blocks around the buildings on the lookout for insurgents and ensuring that these valuable assets belonging to the United States government were not stolen. We were well armed with a baton. No one was going to take any of my buildings.

About three weeks into training, three of us soldiers decided to ask some of the WACs on a group date down to the River Walk in San Antonio, about five miles away. We left the post in a taxi for the River Walk and stopped at the impressive Hilton Palacio del Rio. We ordered drinks and dinner, and everyone got served but Sharon. They forgot her order. After that, the San Antonio River Walk became a special place for us.

The River Walk is a must-visit. It was initially planned in the 1920s to be a covered concrete flood-control channel but was spared by visionary architect Robert Hugman and a vocal group of conservation-minded citizens. It has a series of water passages with restaurants, hotels, and bars on each side; narrow walkways; and beautiful stone bridges. Iconic barges ferried people up and down the river. We liked to sit in the barge, but we did not pay attention to the pilot describing the river and historical sites. We were in love, and it was so nice to be crammed next to her. To this day, my heart warms at the thought of being with Sharon on the River Walk.

I got really brave one Friday at the end of a class on bandaging. Sharon was my partner, and I liked fashioning the shoulder sling on her rather large chest. I picked her up at her barracks, and we walked to a small pizza place on post. We ordered and sat there looking in each other's eyes, starting to see the spark that lights the embers of love. Two hours later, there was still no pizza, and we were the only ones in the pizza shop. They forgot our order!

At about the eighth week of class, with graduation looming, I knew I had to make a move. I asked Sharon for a weekend in downtown San Antonio. She agreed, and I was sailing to the moon. Here I was, a nineteen-year-old guy full of testosterone anticipating a weekend with a twenty-four-year-old beautiful natural blonde. We did not have much money, so we checked in to the Crockett Hotel beside the Alamo. It was built in 1909 and is said to be haunted by the victims of the bloody battles. We did not see nor hear nor care to see or hear any ghosts. We were in the midst of passionate lovemaking that went on and on. We did try to study for our final exams. One subject was anatomy, so we discovered each other's. The Fates wove a strong piece of thread that weekend that remains always within the fabric of my life.

We graduated from 91A school and, sadly, were assigned to different duty stations. She was off to Fort Lee in Virginia to join the Eighty-Fifth Combat Support Battalion. I went to Fort Jackson in South Carolina for my advanced 91C medical training.

# Chapter 9

Who was this woman who had taken my heart?

She grew up in Wisconsin; and she had a stepbrother, Larry, and a sister, Vicky. She was also very shy, so her parents enrolled her in ballet. She took lessons from a Russian former ballerina. Now that's a nice way to help a shy child: put her in front of a stern, stick-carrying instructor.

She loved dance and even made up her own productions with her neighbor Jennine. She made her own projector using a magnifying glass and sold tickets to her events, then she hit up the attendees for additional money for lemonade and pretzels. She knew how to make money even as a child!

She loved cats (we have six), and as a child, she once brought home a frozen carcass. Her mother was appalled but offered, "Let's put the cat by the back, place a blanket over it, and give it some milk. Once the cat warms up, it may go home." Sharon was ecstatic, but once her dad got home, her mother made him dispose of the cat. The next day, Sharon was excited as, obviously, the kitty went home.

Her family moved from conservative Wisconsin to California in the '60s. They experienced a complete culture shock from not only the social environment but the oppressive heat versus the Upper Midwest cold. She went through some very difficult relationships that she never talked about. She married on the rebound an abusive, opioid-dependent man who stayed home drinking while she worked in a bar in Reseda. When the emotional strain became too great, she enlisted, and the Fates wove a thread that changed her life and mine.

# Chapter 10

I was given four weeks of leave before I had to report to Fort Jackson. Sharon went back to California to wrap up some things before reporting to Fort Lee. I walked around town in my Army uniform and cue-ball haircut. Protesters mocked me, but I ignored them. I had stood up to the challenge of serving my country. I wondered if I would ever see my beautiful WAC again. Then out of the blue, a letter came. Sharon needed me to fly to California to help her transport her household goods to Virginia. I jumped at the opportunity.

I was overjoyed to see her again. I met her mother, Inez, and her siblings, Vicky and Larry. Sharon and I rented a small truck, packed it, and headed east on I-40; we crossed eight states and traveled almost 2,600 miles. Since this was pre-GPS, we used the classic AAA TripTik, flipping one page after another.

We would stop for dinner and stay at some small hotel along the interstate. After dinner, we'd go back to our room and make love and have long talks. We would finally fall asleep, wake up the next morning, and start all over again mile after mile. At Fort Lee, we said emotional goodbyes, and I turned south to South Carolina.

Army 91C, Practical Nursing Specialist, was a fifty-two-week course. We were housed two to a room in large barracks next to Moncrief Army Community Hospital. My roommate, Geno, was of Hungarian descent and from Pottstown, Pennsylvania. He had a fiancé back home and liked to drive to see her on weekends. We devised a plan. Friday, with our coursework completed, we packed his car and hit I-95 toward Virginia. He would drop me off at Sharon's apartment then continue to Pottstown.

From Fort Jackson to Fort Lee was about 350 miles; Pottstown was another 299 miles. On Sunday, we arrived back at Fort Jackson in the early hours, got some sleep, and went to class. We did this consistently for almost a year.

Sharon and I were so poor, we did not have a bed, so we pulled the cushions off of the couch and made one. Her IRS refund bought our first bed. We wore it out. We drank cheap Boone's Farm liquor and plotted boundless tomorrows. She continued to tell me I had potential, that I could be someone and do great things. I was skeptical as I had always been told the opposite.

Early in the spring of 1974, I asked her to marry me, and she said yes. I went to the Catholic chaplain at Fort Jackson to discuss marrying this non-Catholic woman. A stern, inflexible colonel, he said he would not marry us unless Sharon converted. I told him, "You can't tell her how or what to do." End of discussion. I called Sharon with the bad news, and she said she'd ask a chaplain at her post. She found Capt. Welch, a young progressive priest, and told him she wanted to get married but that there was an issue.

"So what's the problem, can't find a guy?"

"No," she replied, and then she told him she found a really nice guy but that his chaplain wouldn't perform the ceremony unless she converted.

Welch said he'd get the paperwork going and get us married.

Because Sharon was on active duty, she had to request permission from her commanding officer, and orders had to be cut from the Pentagon. Otherwise, an active-duty female who married could be discharged. We also had to file for two marriage licenses—one from the state of Virginia and one from the Department of Defense.

We planned our wedding for the Labor Day weekend and requested a three-day pass. My parents and brothers took the Greyhound bus from Allentown to Petersburg, Virginia. Sharon planned the entire wedding as a small affair since we had no money. We married on August 31, 1974, at Liberty Chapel on the post at Fort Lee. I went ahead to the chapel with my dad and brothers. Sharon was going to drive to her own wedding with my mother, but the service was delayed when my mom got so anxious that she became physically ill. She finally settled down, and Sharon brought her to the ceremony. My best man was my hot-rodder pal Tommy from Ganci's garage, who came down from Allentown. A vocalist sang "Desiderata" by Max Ehrmann, a prose poem that reflects on how life can be quite a struggle—a concise, inspiring reminder to keep high ideals, treat others kindly, and be gentle with ourselves.

At the end of the ceremony, Capt. Welch signed the marriage license, but there was a problem. Sharon married my dad! His middle initial is *S* while mine is *H*, but the clerk typed in *S* instead of *H*. "No worries," said our unflappable captain. "It will be corrected by Monday morning."

We honeymooned at the Smith Mountain Lake Resort, not far from Fort Lee. I drove back to Fort Jackson, sporting my new wedding ring, which we bought at the PX. I still had five months of 91C training, so initially, we saw each other only weekends. I wrote every day, and so did she. We still have those letters.

I also would call at least twice a week on the barracks pay phone. I already had a guaranteed position at Patterson Army Community Hospital in Fort Monmouth in northern New Jersey. When Sharon received orders to relocate to Fort Monmouth, we were finally together, and the Fates wove another golden thread into my life tapestry.

# Chapter 11

We found an apartment in nearby Hopewell. Fort Monmouth was founded in 1917 as Camp Little Silver and, in the 1940s, became the US Army Signal Corps headquarters. The post featured an interesting high-level security building shaped like a hexagon.

I started at the hospital as a 91C in the ambulance emergency room. I was a member of the EMS and took care of acute and chronic patients. The ambulance ER functioned as a hybrid urgent care and emergency room.

Sharon changed her MOS from basic nursing to psych. She had an associate's degree in psychology from Pierce College in the San Fernando Valley. She qualified as a behavioral science specialist, MOS 91F, and was assigned to the outpatient psych clinic.

Life was good. We were so in love and could not wait to see each other after we got off duty. I was promoted to specialist fifth class and Sharon to specialist fourth class. She took an Army correspondence course on nutrition and dietetics and decided that's what she wanted in a degree once we were discharged for active duty. I intended to stay in the army for twenty years and be a paramedic. Not on her agenda! We took a couple of courses at Brookdale Community College in the evenings as my prep for the ACT.

The post ran a competition for soldier of the month. No member of the hospital unit had ever won as Fort Monmouth was the home of the United States Military Academy Prep School. I entered the competition—an eight-hour ordeal of uniform inspection, military bearing, drill and ceremony, and military knowledge.

I was asked, "Where is building number 1 on post?" The answer? At the base of the flagpole.

What is found on top of the flagpole?

The truck.

What is stored inside the truck?

A razor, a match, a bullet, a grain of rice, and a penny. The items are to be used in case of enemy invasion. If the enemy overwhelms the base, the last survivor must climb the 50- to 75-foot pole, unscrew the truck, strip the flag with the razor, give it a proper retirement with the match, eat the grain of rice for strength, and blind the enemy with the penny. Then the survivor digs up the pistol buried six paces from the base of the pole and shoots himself, so he cannot be taken prisoner.

I was the first from the hospital unit to win the competition. I got to wear a special armband, had reserved parking at the PX, and received all kinds of gift certificates. My hospital commander, Col. Max, was beside himself. He called me into his office and asked what my long-term goals were. I told him the paramedic option, but my wife was dead set against it and wanted me to go big—medical school. He looked at me for a minute and gave some advice: "Listen to the wife. She's always right. Now dismissed."

On June 30, 1976, we were honorably discharged from the US Army. We both received the National Defense Service medal, and I received the Army Commendation Medal. Our household goods were packed, and we were heading west to California. The Fates were extruding a new thread.

# Chapter 12

We moved into a one-bedroom apartment on Prairie Street in Northridge, a few blocks from California State University–Northridge. We could walk to classes. You had to register for each class by going from station to station, picking up a card with the course information, and then proceeding to the computer center to run a schedule. If it synced, you were set. Otherwise, you scrambled for substitute classes. Sharon was working on her last two years for a bachelor's degree in nutrition and dietetics. I was starting the four years for a bachelor's degree in biology for premed. Sharon did not agree with her adviser's degree plan and asked why I even listened to these people. Did they get into medical school? She was correct as usual because in my first semester, I got a D in chemistry. She found in the CSUN catalog a program in environmental and occupational health with interesting classes and the required premed courses fashioned specifically for the degree. I transferred from the College of Science and Mathematics to the College of Health and Human Development. Next semester, I got perfect *A*s. Things were looking up. Medical school now seemed attainable.

I applied to thirty-five medical schools, both DO and MD, and had numerous interviews. I even turned some down. I researched the differences between allopathic (MD) and osteopathic (DO) physicians. Both were recognized and licensed to practice all of the aspects of medicine and surgery.

Andrew Taylor Still, MD, rejected the prevailing system of medical practices throughout the nineteenth century. His techniques relied on anatomical realignment to maintain body homeostasis and healing and to diagnose and treat illness, and he called his practices osteopathy.

What I really liked about the osteopathic philosophy was that it regarded the body as a unit, and the person represents a combination of body, mind, and spirit. The body is capable of self-regulation, self-healing, and health maintenance. Structure and function are reciprocally interrelated. Rational treatment is based on an understanding of these principles: body unity, self-regulation, and the interrelationship of structure and function. In modern medicine, many of the distinctions between allopathic and osteopathic physicians have steadily eroded. All allopathic and osteopathic (DO) physicians train under the same Accrediting Council of Graduate Medical Education (ACGME) programs.

An osteopathic physician is a fully licensed patient-centered physician. A DO has full medical practice rights throughout the United States and in forty-four countries. In the twenty-first century, the training of osteopathic physicians in the United States is equivalent to the training of doctors of medicine (MDs). Osteopathic physicians attend four years of medical school followed by a residency. They use conventional methods of diagnosis and treatment, but with the added training in OMT, the modern derivative of Still's techniques, they work in all specialties.

I was interviewed at the Michigan State University College of Osteopathic Medicine in February, leaving Southern California for sixteen inches of snow. I was interviewed at the University of Minnesota, again in the frigid cold, and did not care for the environment; the students resembled stressed, sun-deprived humanoids. I also was invited to a regional interview with Harvard Medical School. I flew up to San Francisco to meet the dean of admissions, Ogelsby Paul, MD. He was the stereotypical Bostonian with his accent and a bow tie.

Finally, I received some time with the Texas College of Osteopathic Medicine (TCOM) in Fort Worth. It was a fantastic interview. I sensed a different environment—one that felt right.

The rejections came in, but acceptance letters did too. I was accepted at the University of Minnesota, Harvard, and ten other schools. Then came the one I really wanted: TCOM. They sent me an acceptance letter and requested a $100 deposit to hold my place in the class of 1986. I was doing the most improbable thing in my life. I was going to medical school!

I graduated from CSUN with a bachelor's degree in environmental and occupational health. Sharon graduated with an master's degree in nutrition and dietetics. We were off to Texas and the beginning of a tremendously fulfilling career in medicine.

# Chapter 13

The Texas College of Osteopathic Medicine, the first osteopathic medical school in Texas, was founded in 1970 on the fifth floor of Fort Worth Osteopathic Hospital. There were three founders: Drs. Carl Everett, D. D. Byer, and George Leibel, all of whom had an extraordinary vision for a medical school in Fort Worth. In August 1982, I began this lifelong adventure in medical education.

Our class started with hundreds of students, but only 10 percent could be from out of state. I was one of those as I still held a California residency. My out-of-state tuition was $1,500 a semester, easily paid as Sharon was fortunate to immediately land a position as the hospital's chief dietician.

Once we started classes, the information came at a breakneck pace. Our class president was from the Rio Grande Valley, but the class disliked her representation and impeached her. And that's how I became class president.

We followed the traditional curriculum: year 1 was basic science, year 2 was clinical science, year 3 was core clerkships, and year 4 was electives and auditions. I knew I wanted to be a surgeon, so I was excited to start the year 2 surgery course directed by the department founding chair. Dr. Russ was a lanky LBJ look-alike who stood in front of the class and lectured, but he had an annoying habit of jingling his pocket change.

One of the surgery topics was total parenteral nutrition (TPN), which was taught by a junior faculty member. Dr. Sam was frustrated with our class as we could not answer any of his questions, so he stormed out. Being class president, it seemed my duty to approach the chair. I was shaking, but Dr. Russ reassured me he would take care of Dr. Sam. Soon all went back to normal.

Toward the end of the second year, we needed to start planning our core clerkships. No electronic scheduling, of course. Our class met in Med Ed 1, and we filled in the whiteboards. Each board had a rotation, a site, and a required allocation of students. Pandemonium reigned as students filled in the rotations. Some members of the class were distraught when they could not get a particular site and believed their careers were done. I scheduled all my rotations at Fort Worth Osteopathic Hospital, which was where Sharon worked, next to the TCOM campus.

In June 1984, the TCOM class of 1986 was out of the classroom and in the clinical arena. With my military medical training and clinical exposure, I was excited to be back in the clinical environment.

My first rotation was in emergency medicine. Dr. Frank was the preceptor. He worked shifts at the ER and also was pursuing a PhD in education. In slow times, he would take us aside and talk about esoteric, educational "models of mind." We had no clue what he was saying. We thought we were just there to learn emergency medicine.

I was scheduled next for internal medicine and given a list of preceptors. Sharon insisted I rotate with Dr. Pat, but he was a hard grader who rarely gave an *A*. I reluctantly signed up for him, as did a classmate, Student Doctor Kathy.

Dr. Pat would have us do the consult and then present the case to him. We would all go back with him to see the patient, and he would redo the consult. Then we would return to the classroom for discussion. We did this every day for the four-week rotation. Dr. Pat was extremely intelligent; he had two pocket files, one in each pocket of his lab coat, filled to the brim with medical trivia. Today, everything would be accessed by your phone. He called his pocket files his "peripheral brain." I don't think he needed to reference them. I think he thought he looked cool.

One day, when we were going back to redo the consult, he heard a bruit that Kathy did not pick up, so he asked her to listen to the carotid arteries. As she took her stethoscope out of her lab coat, lipstick and makeup flew across the room and hit the patient directly at her right carotid artery. Dr. Pat said, "Well, you found the bruit."

One Friday a month, he would wear a pink shirt and drive his 1971 DeTomaso Pantera. The car was powered by a 5.8-liter (351 cubic inches) Ford Cleveland V8 with a power output of 330 horsepower. It was a chick magnet. Like I said, he thought he was cool.

The chair of the Department of Internal Medicine, Dr. Mike, hired a talented gastroenterologist from Chicago: Dr. Monty. Dr. Monty was into baseball trivia and jokes. He was trained in the early days of more complex GI endoscopy, which was much needed in Fort Worth as patients who required such procedures were always transferred to Dallas. He initially was not welcomed by Dr. Sam, who told him we already had GIs in Fort Worth, but Dr. Monty persevered and became a sought-after gastroenterologist and medical educator.

I did an elective in pulmonary and was assigned another new faculty member straight out of fellowship: Dr. David. It was a great rotation, and I learned a lot that I used throughout my career. He once put me on a ventilator while I was wide awake, so I could feel what it was like being on the different modes. It was not comfortable at all, but he made the point: don't leave a patient on the ventilator overnight just for the doctor's convenience. Year 4 came along, and soon I was gone four months for elective and audition rotations, which were real-time interviews of medical knowledge, problem solving, and fit for a program.

My first out-rotation was at Doctors Hospital in Columbus, Ohio. I elected to do a thoracic-vascular rotation with Dr. Richard, who was somewhat egocentric and wore white scrubs, his name and titles embroidered in red. "Why do I wear all white?" he asked once. I did not have an answer, so he told me. "Only the pope can wear all white." It was a very busy service—two or three thoracotomies and maybe eight vascular cases a week. It was a notable rotation for volume, scope, and variety. On the last day, Dr. Richard took me to a nice restaurant for dinner and called Sharon from Ohio on his bag phone to tell her I did well on his service.

My next audition was at Grandview Medical Center in Dayton, Ohio, to do an elective cardiology. My preceptor, Dr. James G., was from Houston and wore custom cowboy boots with the state of Texas in silver on the toe, Houston marked in ruby red. We rounded after noon, then we were off to the cardiac cath lab (cardiac catheterization lab) until evening.

Dr. James G. had a few acres of farmland outside Dayton with a full-sized caboose on the property as well as the little red brick schoolhouse his grandparents attended, completely restored. He also had a covered bridge he had preserved, and that became an Ohio landmark. I was there when the governor dedicated it.

My last audition rotation at Tulsa Regional Medical Center in Tulsa, Oklahoma, excited me as it was designated cardiothoracic, which was my preferred specialty. Tulsa Regional Medical Center sits at the junction of two freeways, so receiving level 2 and 3 trauma was common. The facility had residencies and fellows in almost all aspects of medicine including ENT and ophthalmology. Sharon wanted me to be an ophthalmologist, but I had no interest in doing cataracts all day (little did I envision LASIK).

My rotation in cardiothoracic surgery went very well. I interacted with the general surgery residents as I needed to do a full general surgery residency prior to cardiothoracic. In cardiothoracic surgery, you do a formal residency, not a fellowship; otherwise, you can't qualify for boards. For every other specialty, you do a base program followed by a fellowship.

I interviewed prior to leaving my rotation and had a good feeling that this was where I would start postgraduate training. The director of medical education called and said I was selected as an intern for the academic year 1986–87. A contract soon followed. The intern stipend was $16,000.

I returned to Fort Worth and completed the last semester. We had a dinner the night before graduation, and all the academic honors were announced. I received the internal medicine, surgery, and pediatric awards. I missed number 1 in my class by 0.36 percent.

Family members were there from Allentown. My dad was in a good phase. Sharon's family came from San Antonio and California. Sharon arranged a nice dinner at the Worthington Hotel in downtown Fort Worth. She had saved money on two consulting jobs and bought me a beautiful watch. As I walked across the stage, I went from being Mr. Yurvati to Dr. Yurvati. Never could I have imagined such a moment. I now had become a provider. The Fates wove this golden thread into my life and linked it to the love of my life's tapestry as well.

We packed up and moved to Tulsa for five years of training in general surgery.

# Chapter 14

We found a condo on Eighty-Fifth Street across from Oral Roberts University. We could see the tall golden prayer tower out the window.

Orientation was on the last week of June 1986, and I was on call as an intern on July 1. Our director of medical education, Dr. Fred, required all interns to wear baby-blue lab coats, so everyone knew we were newbies. Each of us was linked with a buddy intern; mine was Bobbie from Kansas, and he wanted to be an orthopedic surgeon.

I was given the solemn privilege over life and death as a new provider of healthcare. Talk about scary! On the first night, I had to intubate, prep a patient for a laparotomy, and fix every constipated bowel in the hospital.

We all were required to do a PGY1 rotating internship, which included pediatrics and OB-GYN. While I was on pediatrics, Bobbie's wife came to the obstetrics suite in labor and required a C-section. Pediatrics was always at C-sections to take care of the newborn immediately after delivery. We delivered a healthy baby, and I absconded with the scissors used to cut the cord (after a correct instrument count). I later had the scissors gold-plated and mounted, and I attached a small engraved plaque noting date and time of delivery.

Intern year went by rapidly. I was interviewed for the general surgery program and was accepted. July 1 came around, and I was on call on my first night as a surgical resident. Two bowel obstructions went to the OR. The next morning, my program director called, very upset. I operated with Dr. Hans, but the referrals should have gone to the program director's group. How was I to know? It also was a new emergency medicine resident who called for the consults. He got over it after I explained that the ER called the consults. Shortly after that, a memo came out listing primary care referrals to surgeons in the training program.

I did an elective out-rotation at the University of Nebraska with Dr. Budd, a leading liver transplant surgeon. One of his faculty, Dr. Alan, was a DO. He taught me a tremendous amount of transplant physiology, pharmacology, and management. I did consider a possible transplant fellowship, but CT surgery was my calling.

My second out-rotation was in cardiothoracic surgery at the Deborah Heart and Lung Center in Browns Mills, New Jersey. Deborah has an extraordinary story beginning with its founding in 1922 as a tuberculosis sanatorium and pulmonary center. Lore has it that the therapeutic air of rural Burlington County was key to patient recovery. With antibiotic medications soon leading to the eradication of TB, Deborah's focus widened to other chest diseases. When pioneering physician Dr. Charles Bailey performed Deborah's first open-heart surgery, an off-pump mitral stenosis, the specialty of cardiac diseases, was immediately embraced, transforming Deborah into New Jersey's only cardiac and pulmonary specialty hospital.

My interview was scrubbing with the chief of surgery, Dr. Lynn. He was very intense, wasted no time, and expected instant responses from his staff. He went to medical school in Nova Scotia followed by a surgical residency in Canada. He redid all of his training in the US at the Brigham and Women's Hospital in Boston, then he took a cardiothoracic residency at the University of Alabama under the brilliant cardiac surgeon John Kirklin.

We handled three cases of tetralogy of Fallot and five adult cardiac cases during my interview. I did call with the CT resident in the CVICU. I was up all night managing cases while he slept. I found out later that he was being paid by the intensivist group.

At the end of the month, I was offered a position as a cardiothoracic and vascular resident. The board requires two years of cardiothoracic training, but this particular program took three years as vascular surgery was integrated into it. So I went back to Oklahoma to tell Sharon the good news and the not so good: I had to face another three years of training.

We had a graduation from the Tulsa Regional / Oklahoma State University general surgery program, and the next day, I did my last case with Dr. Larry, the chief of ENT. Sharon was not pleased. I had graduated and should have been done with the program.

# Chapter 15

In New Jersey, I lived in one of the on-site apartments for house staff. I hit the ground running; and since we had no duty-hour restrictions, it was eat, drink, and sleep surgery. Dr. Joe, Dr. Walter, and I made a strong team. The cardiac service was purring.

Three months later, Sharon joined me, and we found a rental house in neighboring Marlton. She was hired as the chief dietician, and we were now settled for the next three years.

In the fall of my second year, we went to Lithuania to do pediatric cardiac surgery funded by the Children of the World Foundation. In one week, we saw twenty-five children. Most had simple atrial septal defects, some had ventricular, and one needed tricuspid repair. It was a real experience: Russia had granted independence to the Baltic states, and I got a firsthand look at a failed socialist system—no supplies, few resources, and professionals driving taxis as there were no positions for them. Whereas we stayed at a large hotel and were bused every morning to the hospital, our chief had a driver around the clock and a car. I lost fifteen pounds during that trip. Our chief had our scrub techs carry the instruments on the plane because once we arrived back in New Jersey, we had cases lined up the next day. Forget jet lag.

At the completion of the program, I logged 1,200 cardiac, 250 pediatric, 275 major thoracic, and 185 vascular cases.

I found a cardiac staff position in Michigan, joining a group founded by my prior chief surgery resident from Tulsa, Dr. JD. All my years of training were finally complete, and I was transitioning into an actual provider.

# Chapter 16

Finally, my first position as a cardiac surgeon in Lansing, Michigan. I joined two surgeons, Dr. JD and Dr. Greg. I was on call every other week and weekend (they did every third). This arrangement was to help me build a practice, and that it did. I was getting cases and consults, the nurses were referring family, and the partners were not pleased as they thought they should be the center of attention.

Winters in Michigan are overcast with almost daily lake-effect snow. Thankfully, our house in East Lansing was on the same street as the mayor, so we always had our street plowed. We liked living there, but my group was dysfunctional; after about two years, I left. I considered starting my own practice and explored this with the hospital system. My former partners were in with the board and the CEO, though, and the system withdrew the offer. I was now unemployed as a cardiac surgeon!

Ah, but TCOM in Fort Worth had just started a new cardiac program and needed a second surgeon. Sharon and I flew to Fort Worth, and it was like homecoming. Everyone was excited to see us, and the interview went well. I was offered a position at $175,000 a year. So it was time to pack up and move south to better weather. It was a good decision to escape the toxic environment and start anew. It felt like we were heading to a wonderful place that would enable me to have a wonderful career.

# Chapter 17

We found a home in Southlake, an upscale community north of Fort Worth and close to DFW Airport. I joined Dr. Bill in the professional building next to the hospital. We provided all of the cardiac and thoracic services to support the cardiology program.

One week after starting my new position, Dr. Bill left for a one-week vacation. Fresh out of training, I'm on my own. My first case was an unstable LAD dissection out of the cath lab, and to complicate things, she had bilateral Halstedian mastectomies and cobalt radiation to the chest in the 1950s. She did well post-op, and over the years, we did bilateral carotid endarterectomies and femoral-popliteal bypasses on her. Her sternotomy took three years to heal. It was quite an endeavor involving wound vacs and split-thickness skin grafting.

I started to build a referral base and was doing open heart surgeries and some thoracic and vascular cases. About two years later, I was covering the weekend for my partner when a lady he had operated on for spinal exposure developed an incomplete bowel obstruction that eventually became ischemic bowel. A few days later, she died. We received notice of a malpractice claim—my introduction to the arena of tort.

At my deposition, I learned what and how to answer questions without getting trapped. Eventually, we were in the courtroom, trying the case before a judge and jury. It was not pleasant. I had seen the lady one weekend and never operated on her, but the plaintiff's attorney kept me on the stand for a solid week. The jury went into deliberation after three weeks of testimony, and during this time, we were approached to settle. I held out, and our attorneys kept pressuring us. When the jury could not agree on a verdict and the judge granted a mistrial, the plaintiffs immediately filed for a retrial. I found a different attorney to defend just me. My big error had been sharing litigators with my partner. I held out and was summarily dismissed; he paid a multimillion-dollar settlement.

I was not happy in private practice. I wanted more of an academic career, but TCOM did not have a surgery opening. I secured a research opportunity in the Department of Integrative Physiology with Dr. Perter, who had NASA and NIH grants. I would go to the lab and line up subjects with an arterial catheter and a central line then head off to my day in the OR or in the office. The lab was robust, and I was coauthor on multiple publications.

Around this time, I started to collaborate with Dr. Bob, who was using an isolated guinea pig heart to study pyruvate as an energy source, a free-radical scavenger, and for its positive hemodynamic effects. I proposed that we obtain a heart-lung machine and put some pigs on bypass.

# Chapter 18

Pyruvate is an important compound in biochemistry, the output of the metabolism of glucose, which is known as glycolysis. One molecule of glucose breaks down into two molecules of pyruvate, which are then used to provide further energy in one of two ways. Pyruvate is converted into acetyl coenzyme A, which is the main input for a series of reactions known as the Krebs cycle (or citric acid cycle or tricarboxylic acid cycle, because citric acid is one of the intermediate compounds formed during the reactions). Pyruvate is also converted to oxaloacetate, which replenishes Krebs cycle intermediates; also, the oxaloacetate is used for gluconeogenesis. These reactions are named after Hans Krebs, the biochemist awarded the 1953 Nobel Prize for physiology, jointly with Fritz Lipmann, for research into metabolic processes. We received a large grant to continue our research. We took our data and obtained an IRB-approved clinical trial, and the results were fantastic.

If insufficient oxygen is available, the acid is broken down anaerobically, creating lactate. Pyruvate from glycolysis pyruvate is a key intersection in the network of metabolic pathways. Bob had studied this compound as a postdoc and is considered a leading expert on pyruvate, so we modified a cardioplegia solution, which is used to arrest the heart on bypass. We did this on a series of pigs and found positive effects of the compound on the arrested heart. From that work, we obtained another grant to study the molecular biology and mechanism of how pyruvate protected the heart while arrested and how the heart recovered faster after bypass.

We have been fortunate to train some excellent DO/PhD students in the lab. All found competitive residencies and have become proficient clinicians/scientists.

# *Chapter 19*

The Fates continue to weave your life threads. What are the chances that you're admitted to a medical school and given opportunities to save lives? It was a Friday afternoon, and I received a STAT call from the cath lab: Dr. Marty has a ninety-year-old patient with an acute MI that the LAD dissected during the angioplasty, and the patient needed urgent cardiac surgery. Oh, by the way, the patient is Dr. Carl, one of the TCOM founders! We completed a triple bypass and utilized every agent we'd been researching in our lab—aprotinin to reduce bleeding, thyroid hormone to improve cardiac function, and a whole lot of luck. You will be remembered for either saving the founder or losing the patient. Well, Dr. Carl had a remarkable recovery and lived to age ninety-seven.

A year later, a call came from the lab, saying that my former dean, the man who signed my diploma, needed an aortic valve replacement for severe aortic stenosis. So off we went to the OR and successfully replaced Dr. T Eugene's aortic valve. What are the chances that you're admitted to a medical school and operate on a founder *and* your dean? The Fates surely were testing me. In cardiac surgery, you either succeed or fail. There is no in-between.

All of the procedures were completed at one of the last stand-alone osteopathic hospitals in the state—the Osteopathic Medical Center of Texas. The hospital closed on October 8, 2004, sending out one thousand employees, three hundred physicians, and sixty interns and residents to find employment with barely twenty-four hours' notice. I was the last chief of the medical staff. I removed the plaque from the fifth floor, which noted the foundation of TCOM, and hustled it out of the building past the security guards hired to keep people like me from doing things like that. I also stealthily removed the gavel used by every chief of staff from 1946. Both items can be found at the University of North Texas Health Science Center in the rare books room.

The medical staff scattered to other hospitals in Fort Worth. My cardiothoracic practice and all the postgraduate training programs moved to Plaza Medical Center, now Medical City Fort Worth, an HCA hospital. MCFW has a designated cardiovascular OR on the fourth floor, well way from the main OR. I took over room 2 and built a vigorous thoracic surgical practice with referrals from the nearby towns of Weatherford and Granbury. We were doing over 120 major thoracic procedures annually and were the go-to thoracic oncology unit.

# Chapter 20

## The Xiphoid Story

Let me tell you about the xiphoid story. I was referred a high school basketball player who was experiencing severe substernal pain around the xiphoid (cartilage at the base of the sternum, the lump at the end of the breastbone). I was doctor number 13 and diagnosed a little-known condition: xiphoidalgia. I recommended to the parents a surgical excision of the cartilage, and the results were remarkable. Their daughter rejoined the Brock High School team, which subsequently won back-to-back state championships.

This index case caused an explosion of referrals. UNTHSC placed a video on YouTube, and any search for xiphoid pain or xiphoidalgia tagged me. Soon, we were getting calls from all over the US and other countries; patients who had suffered for years and failed multiple therapies were coming to Fort Worth for the surgery. A notable patient from the Netherlands, a military sniper, was experiencing pain at the xiphoid area when positioning prone. We received permission as the experts in this surgery from the US Department of Defense and the Royal Netherlands Marines. The sniper did remarkably, and his accuracy improved 100 percent.

We published the world's largest series of xiphoid surgeries in the journal *International Surgery*. The final count was over ninety procedures, and countless patients either improved or were completely pain free.

A blues guitar player from Colorado, Zakk DeBono, found us on YouTube and came to Fort Worth. The guitar was causing xiphoidal pressure. Now he is completely cured, and his career took off. He is so talented that I foresee recording contracts and a future Grammy!

# Chapter 21

One perhaps never expects to attain international notoriety. My first contact with Professor Terry was at a Society of Thoracic Surgery meeting in San Antonio. I was investigating leucocyte filtration and cardiopulmonary bypass in reducing post-operative atrial fibrillation. This complication occurs in about 25 percent of patients post-bypass, believed to be due to inflammation. I developed a protocol combining leukocyte filtration (mechanical) and aprotinin (pharmacological), and atrial fibrillation dropped dramatically to 8 percent.

My filtration representative introduced me to Professor Terry, who invited me to present a poster at the annual therapeutic filtration and extracorporeal circulation (TFEC) conference in London at the famous Hammersmith Hospital. I had never been to London, so I thought this would be an appropriate meeting to attend. About three weeks prior, Professor Terry called and said a speaker was ill and that he desperately needed me to present as speaker. It required me to convert the poster to a full-length manuscript as the proceedings would be published in the journal *Perfusion*. And Professor Terry's secretary, Karen, would not allow me in the meeting without the manuscript ready to go! So I dutifully converted the poster to a manuscript, and I was off to my first UK visit.

The meeting was in an old auditorium with wooden benches and floor. I presented, and there was silence. Professor Kent, the head of the department and a prominent cardiac surgeon (aprotinin is dosed by the "Hammersmith dosing," which he developed), stood up, and I expected to be hammered. Instead, he hammered his people, asking why they had not thought of my scheme. I was overwhelmed. The speakers' dinner that evening was delightful. I was invited back each year to present and ultimately served as a moderator. Professor Terry obtained a visiting professorship for me at the Imperial College in London. I was there for the London bombing last July 7, 2005. It was surreal to experience London shut down and actually quiet.

Professor Terry left the Imperial College and returned to his home in Glasgow, Scotland, and to the University of Strathclyde, where he received his PhD. He arranged a visiting professorship for me there too; I was the first DO since the founding of the university in 1796. We continue to develop collaborative research between UNTHSC and Strathclyde.

Whenever Professor Terry comes over, he insists on staying at the "Yurvati estate" as he loves our fantastic garden. I have taken him to the Fort Worth Stockyards, Billy Bob's Texas, and other venues. At Billy Bob's, I got him to sit in the judges' area above the chutes; he was fascinated that you could wrap a cord around a bull's balls and ride him. Pure Texas!

On one of his visits, we went to the President's Ball, a university fundraiser. He wore his full kilt, and I wore a tuxedo. We looked like the Highlander and James Bond. He went outside for a smoke, and next to him was another gentleman in a kilt who looked at Terry and asked if he was there for a wedding. Terry said "No, mate, I am really from Scotland."

Our UNTHSC-Strathclyde collaborations explore combining their mechanical devices with our supercharged tissue preservation and energy solutions. Our teams hypothesize that we can preserve injured limbs from soldiers on the battlefield and reduce the amputation rate significantly. This is such a rewarding aspect of my career.

# Chapter 22

We were taught in medical school that painless hematuria is cancer until proven otherwise. Sharon had two episodes of hematuria; her primary care was aggressive and obtained cultures and a CT scan of the kidneys, and nothing showed other than lots of red blood cells in the urine. Next, we went for a cystoscopy. The cystoscopy photos were very concerning for the starburst effect at the dome of the bladder (I have seen the same pattern on the surface of the lung in patients with adenocarcinoma). Pathology reported urachal adenocarcinoma, a rare tumor—one in 5 million—with a 32 percent chance of surviving five years. I got to tell her as the urologist called me with the report. We both cried, sitting together on the couch, wondering how and why.

Our oncology friend Dr. Bibbas referred us to an oncologic urologist who trained at MD Anderson, and we planned a robot-assisted partial cystectomy. We had already scheduled a trip to Atlantis in the Bahamas, so we did that. And upon our return, she underwent surgical resection. The tumor was staged as a T3b fat invasion, but the staging system was base 1 bladder cancer; the urachus was all fatty remnant on the dome of the bladder, so a direct correlation was difficult. She did well and surpassed the five years, and now she is into the seven-year survival category.

She undergoes a cystoscopy and CT abdomen/pelvis every other year. Thus far, she is disease free—a true survivor.

# Chapter 23

Our fortieth anniversary was spent on an amazing escapade in the South Pacific. We went from Texas to Los Angeles, traveled from Los Angeles to Tahiti, then took a fifty-minute flight to Bora Bora. We stayed at the Four Seasons in a bungalow over the water. It was so peaceful and relaxing. We did a Jet Ski tour around the atoll with Sharon insisting on driving. We did an underwater scooter (like an open submarine with a pressurized canopy) that was phenomenal and rode a 4x4 up the mountain. Incongruously, cannons recycled from a World War I battleship had been hauled up the mountain to guard the inlet. Even better, they were engraved with the place of origin—Bethlehem Steel! The forges were in Bethlehem, Pennsylvania, next to Allentown. Here was a military artifact from my home area over six thousand miles away.

For our forty-fifth anniversary, we intended to take a trip to Hawaii, but there were obstacles. First, the volcano erupted, then a hurricane hit the islands. And then Sharon became very concerned that these were signs. "If I go to Hawaii, I will die," she announced a week before our departure. I immediately called our agent, Margi, who was able to book flights and accommodations to the Mandarin Oriental in Canouan Island, St. Vincent and the Grenadines. This resort was unreal. We had a 1,700-square-foot villa, all marble and high-end woods. We were one of four couples, then two, then just us, and our hosts treated Sharon like a princess. We had our own valet, Lennie, who arranged the daily Mercedes SUV to the private beach. Dinners were indescribably good. Even our return trip to St. Lucia was first class via the resort's private jet. We had such a grand time, but because of the late changes, we cut one day off to reduce expenses.

The morning of September 5, 2018, changed our lives and began transforming me from a provider to a caregiver. At 3:30 a.m., when I usually went to exercise prior to my surgery schedule, I could not rouse Sharon. Limp and incoherent, she was having a massive stroke. I called 911, and the paramedics wanted to take her to the closest hospital, Baylor Grapevine. I held firm for Medical City Fort Worth, a designated NIH stroke center. After some discussion, the paramedic said he needed permission form the medical director. He was a former student of mine, and he gave the green light.

I called the ER, and they mobilized the stroke team. By the time I arrived, she was in the neuro interventional lab. With the first dye blush, my heart sank. There was no blood flow to her left brain. Thankfully, the doctors retrieved a one-centimeter clot from her middle cerebral artery and reestablished blood flow. She was transferred back to the neuro ICI, and I went to remove an eight-pound tumor from a man's chest.

After the surgery, I visited the ICU, and she was waking up. Her sister, Vicky, had arrived from San Antonio and had that deer-in-the-headlights look, trying to process what happened. On day 3, Sharon was transferred to the neuro stepdown and then to inpatient rehab. In three and a half weeks, she was home, slept often, had some lower-extremity weakness and significant expressive aphasia.

We arranged for outpatient rehab with PT, OT, and speech therapy, but it did not last long as she got frustrated with the PT/OT (but liked the speech therapist). The biggest mistake was trying to make her bake a brownie package mix. I tried to get the OT to follow Sharon's Betty Crocker children's cookbook recipe, but no, Sharon had to read and comprehend the directions on a package mix. This did not bode well. She dismissed the PT and OT, and the rehab director would not cooperate and allow speech therapy only, saying the program is comprehensive; it's all three elements or none. That ended the in-home rehab. Sharon was on her own.

I was now a caregiver. If I did not cook, she could not remember to eat. I took over paying the bills (yes, actual paper checks) and taxes and running a monthly budget (she always did that; I just brought home the money). I had started working remotely from my library pre-COVID-19, so transitioning to total closure was not disruptive. I had to be home for any repairman or deliveries as she was (still is) reluctant to talk with people she does not know. I had to adjust clinic and surgery schedules. I leave work earlier to be with her and ensure she is safe.

We have made considerable progress in spite of the lingering expressive aphasia, which is both verbal and written. Book 5 of her *Chroma Crossing Chronicles* is still in her computer; she was working on some edits and wrapping up the story. Now I just power up the battery once a month.

With her neurocognitive status at a plateau, I transferred care from her PCP to UNTHSC Geriatrics, a premier center of excellence for age-related neurocognitive disorders. The programs are under the direction of a dynamic fireball—Dr. JK.

We are trialing a medication, rivastigmine, using a twenty-four-hour delivery patch. The drug is used to treat memory loss associated with mild, moderate, or severe Alzheimer's disease. After a brain injury such as ischemic stroke, the risk of dementia increases. One of the earliest and biggest changes is a decrease in the chemical acetylcholine (ACh). ACh helps the brain work properly. Rivastigmine is an acetylcholinesterase inhibitor that slows the breakdown of ACh and may yield improvement in neurocognitive function. We're hoping for even minor progress. I think if we see that, Sharon will be motivated. It's a tough one, rewiring a blonde brain!

I have witnessed some minor changes like some complete, coherent sentences. She started to reread a book she read prestroke, now going on two years.

I manage to get home early every Friday to take her to dinner and maybe run errands, anything to get her out of the house. Sometimes an urgent surgery hits the emergency room, and she's disappointed. But I make it up to her the following Friday. You just ignore the ER calls when you are not on "ER call." We were getting used to this routine, then a global pandemic shut everything down. This did not help her aphasia as she had no new neuro stimuli, and she regressed. She would open up after a visit from her sister or a short shopping trip with her friend Maggie.

Physical aspects—dexterity, ambulation, driving reflexes—either were little affected to begin with or have returned. Her motor skills came back rapidly (she's left-handed, so right brain mobility). However, the stroke being on the left took out Broca's speech center, so her speech is messy. She processes speech coming in, but it's mixed coming out. This frustrates her.

She's really trying to break through her expressive aphasia to the point of spelling words or doing charades in order for me to understand her. Being together for over forty years, you sometimes telepathically know what the other is thinking or saying.

Caregiver—it's my second job. The Fates tied two cords, Sharon's and mine, to complicate our lives. I would be tied to no one else.

# Chapter 24

My John Deere was on its last leg. A piece of metal from the cowling ruptured and blew through the side. So I decided one Friday to stop at Lowe's and buy a new little tractor.

The guy who sold it to me said he would deliver it for free if he could have my old one. He likes to rebuild these things, so I thought, *Why not?* We agreed for him to drop it off after he left work. He arrived in his pickup. Unloading the new tractor was demanding but doable. Loading my old tractor did not go as well. With an over-sized rear transmission, all of the weight was in the back; the tractor shifted, so I pulled with all of my strength to get the wheels on the truck bed. The awful pain started about twelve hours later.

I thought I had a back strain or ruptured disc. Our OMM expert, Dr. Ryan, diagnosed a torn psoas muscle and severe lumbar muscle spasm. Treatments helped but only temporarily. As symptoms worsened, I started to have burning radicular pain down the nerve tracks. I could hardly walk to the kitchen. I wanted to stay flat as that lessened the pressure on my spine. The pain got so bad that I found some old hydromorphone tablets that Sharon had for her back pain, and even that didn't help. Now I know why patients with severe extremity vascular compromise begged me to take off their limbs. There is no relief for this pain.

God alone knows how I actually did an emergency case. It was a long-standing patient, Norma Jean; I must have done fifteen-plus surgeries on her and salvaged her life, with the grace of God, multiple times. I knew the family and had been invited each year to Thanksgiving dinner and their house. I was their "concierge surgeon." I could not foresee that hers was the last surgery I would ever do.

I continued to try and work, thinking it was a ruptured disc. I finally gave in and called my PCP, who also is the TCOM dean, and requested an MRI. I drove twenty-one miles downtown in debilitating pain and then, because of COVID-19, had to come back in three hours! I went up to my clinical office and crashed on the couch until it was my appointment time. The radiologist, whom I have known over fifteen years, completed the read on the MRI. "So it's a really bad ruptured disc," I said. You know it's not good when they don't look you in the eye. Dr. Paul said, "No, it's a pathological fracture of the third lumbar vertebra." It's completely destroyed, and I have cord compression. That's what's causing the radicular nerve pain.

# Chapter 25

In the blink of an eye, the Fates had cut some of my life cords. A pathological fracture means cancer. I have cancer in the bone marrow—multiple myeloma. I went from being a provider who becomes a caregiver to being a caregiver who becomes a patient.

Multiple myeloma is a cancer of the plasma cells, which are a type of white blood cells that produce antibodies. It occurs with a 0.76 percent incidence, or 1.8 percent of all cancers. With current treatment regimens, five-year survival is estimated at 54 percent. The disease can be controlled, but *there is no cure*. That's not something a thoracic surgeon wants to hear. I remove tumors and cure cancer. I don't "leave it in place."

Dr. Paul gave me two options: minimally invasive kyphoplasty or traditional open fusion with fixation. The latter would take me out for weeks. Who would care for my patients?

I went home and crashed flat in bed to take the pressure off of my spine. I texted Sharon's oncologist, Dr. Bibbas, with my reports. The next morning, he called, so apologetic for not seeing the reports the night before. I was in such pain, my legs were on fire, and I could hardly stand to use the bathroom. He offered me a direct admit for pain control, and by then, I was ready for anything. I said, "Sure, let me get dressed and drive in," and he said, "No way, I'm picking you up." I rode lying down in his Tesla. Every bump felt like a bomb detonating in my back.

I was directly admitted to my stepdown floor at Medical City Fort Worth, my go-to hospital. We repeated my MRI and completed a skeletal survey, looking for other myeloma sites. High-dose opioids finally took the edge off of my pain. I now waited through the weekend (nothing happens in a hospital on weekends!) and spent my sixty-fifth birthday there. Due to COVID-19, Sharon could not visit. I ordered myself a birthday present, a watch, and waited for a decision.

On Monday, Interventional Radiology took a pass on the kyphoplasty—too risky, given the cord compression. Back to square one. We waited for the neurosurgeon, and we finally agreed on multilevel fusion. He said I would be his second case tomorrow; I retorted, "Hey, move me up to first." Everything was now in motion; my favorite anesthetists saw me for pre-op, and we were scheduled for 6:30 the next morning.

The surgery lasted five and a half hours. I woke up in the recovery room. I had no pulse in my right foot and a cool, white leg. *Damn,* I thought, *arterial thrombosis with an occlusion.* It turned out to be severe vasospasm, which we eased with warm air via a Behr hugger. I was transferred back to my room, but the cardiovascular nurses were not comfortable managing a post-op spinal fusion, so I received a VIP suite on the neuro floor.

On post-op day 1, I tried to move, and the back spasms almost took me out. My appetite was dreadful for the next few days, and I got severely constipated from the opioids. I felt like a tic ready to explode. My OMM guys came by and did a mesenteric release, which finally got things moving. What a relief to finally take a dump.

One late night, I had to urinate so badly, so I picked up the urinal in the dark but could not get it in. What the hell was going on? I was so high on opioids that I did not realize the lid was still on. You take your humor where you find it.

We started physical therapy almost immediately, and quickly I went from walker to cane. Maybe I had aged fifteen years over six weeks, but I was *not* going to resemble an old man. I got my first shower, and it was like a gift from heaven. I had not shaved in forever and looked like El Chapo. I was waiting for the FBI to show up at my room. Six days later, I left the hospital. The CEO called an Uber ride. Truly, it was a relief to get home.

# Chapter 26

I bought a mechanical grabber. It is a law of physics that when you're not supposed to bend or stoop, you drop everything. Many other adjustments followed as I started to heal. I consulted a good friend and CCHS classmate, Dr. George (you remember; he got us beer), who specializes in spine rehab; he has written many of the protocols for the minimally invasive procedures. His rehab instructions were excellent; you could feel the difference postexercise. The results initially were short-lived, but as I continued recovery, the regimen really kicked in. Way to go, George!

Next up was medical oncology and a plan for treating this devastating disease. Working with Dr. Bibbas and the Center for Cancer and Blood Disorders in Fort Worth, we mapped out an FDA-approved three-drug protocol for multiple myeloma: Darzalex (IV), Revlimid (oral), and Prednisolone (oral)—a weekly infusion for ten weeks then biweekly for another cycle.

The IV infusion was tricky. You had to pretreat with a bolus of steroids and Benadryl. Darzalex is a monoclonal antibody, and an anaphylactic reaction could take you out. Then the infusion is slow—over five or six hours. For those of you who know me, hyper Al sitting still for that length of time is unfathomable. But I persisted and completed the initial cycle. My labs stayed stable (no hair loss even), although fatigue and weakness appeared by day's end. I better tolerated the biweekly cycle. Good news: I responded to the treatment, and all markers went down. I was now in remission.

I was at Baylor Medical Center in Dallas for a bone marrow transplant. Dr. Brian, its leading bone marrow transplant physician, and I devised a rather complicated way to harvest my stem cells for contingencies.

You receive the drug Filgrastim for four days in a row, and it stimulates your bone marrow to put out white blood cells and stem cells. A large-bore dual-lumen catheter was attached onto my subclavian vein for the plasmapheresis to extract stem cells. On day five, you're attached to the plasmapheresis machine for five hours. My harvested white blood cell count was sixty-one thousand (normal range being five to ten thousand), and in one setting, we extracted 3.1 million stem cells—enough for two bone marrow transplants. We're keeping them frozen with the hope we never use them.

# Chapter 27

Everything seemed to be going in the right direction until suddenly I developed severe left leg and thigh pain so extreme that I was unable to sleep. An MRI revealed inflammation from the implanted hardware and a trapped sciatic nerve. Two nerve blocks gave only temporary relief, so the next option was a dorsal column stimulator. Two implanted leads attached to a pacemaker-type battery transmit a signal to block pain. We had to wait for approval and then do a ten-day trial. Temporary leads were attached to an external control box. Everything worked, but I could not shower for ten days! The successful trial earned me precertification for the actual implant. I had to go to a surgery center for the procedure, and all went well. This device, easily recharged via a transcutaneous charger, is life-changing.

The device has artificial intelligence, and after a month, it learns supine, standing, sitting, and walking and can preactivate. For me, it meant glorious relief, increased activity, fewer opioids, and finally, uninterrupted sleep. Only thing left was the sacroiliac joint issue. But 70 percent of patients who undergo a spinal fusion get sacroiliac joint dysfunction. The treatment is a minimally invasive pinning of the joint.

# Chapter 28

Well, the SI joint pinning is officially on hold. The Fates have done it again! I woke up on November 1, 2020, the day after Halloween, a blue moon and the time change. I went to the dishwasher to pull out the cats' food dishes and could not move my right arm; I could not grasp. I first thought I was having a stroke, but with the arm pain and my hand turning white with no pulse, I knew, instead, it was an acute arterial occlusion of my arm. I called my friend Dr. Joe, and we went to the Medical City Fort Worth ER, mobilizing Interventional Radiology on the way.

I went immediately to the IR lab, and the angiogram revealed a few-centimeter blood clot in my right auxiliary artery. An infusion catheter was attempted for a few hours with clot-busting drugs. When I went back to the lab later that day and the artery had not cleared, I went to the OR for a thrombectomy by my colleague Dr. Jim, a most trusted cardiothoracic surgeon.

All looked fine until the next day. My right foot had lost pulses. A new clot formed in my right leg, and I went back to the OR for a second thrombectomy. It was a rough incision below the knee, and post-op, my leg blew up like a balloon—what we call reperfusion edema. In a research project from our lab, we had developed a solution to rescue this complication, but it was experimental and not FDA approved. I feared this meant more surgery for a fasciotomy or, worse, an amputation. However, we elevated my leg on eight pillows, and the edema slightly resolved. I was placed on oral blood thinners and blessedly got discharged. Home recovery using a walker took about four weeks to get the swelling down.

# Chapter 29

At long last, a pain-free norm was dawning. The high-stress chaos was behind us.

No, it was not. The Fates wove another thread.

I had LASIK in 2010 and was doing fine until ten years later. While dealing with my cancer, I noticed difficulty driving at night; I was seeing halos around lights and had foggy vision. I figured it was medication induced, but my PCP said, "You didn't pay attention in ophthalmology. You have cataracts." He was correct. My ophthalmologist diagnosed grade 3 cataracts. Steroid-induced cataracts are rare, but the progression is aggressive. My vision had declined in just a few months to a brown film, muted colors, and a lack of texture.

The ophthalmologist who did my LASIK, Dr. Brian, recommended (Medicare does not cover) the trifocal PanOptix lens. It gave excellent results: vibrant colors, fantastic textures, no more readers. I can even see better driving at night. I had slight astigmatism in my right eye and went in for an old-fashioned PRK, and my vision is fantastic now, twenty-twenty.

# Chapter 30

I still had persistent severe low back pain from the cancer in my third lumbar spine vertebra (L3), so we were going to trial external beam radiation therapy (XRT). I hoped my optimistic radiation oncologist was right as I wanted to get back into training and running. Getting fat from the steroids limited my activity, and I missed the last two Cowtown Marathons.

The process is simple, and it starts with a CT scan for planning. The radiation oncologist and the medical physicist use the scan to determine how much radiation is needed, how long the beam opens, and how many fractions (visits) are needed. We planned ten fractions. They were very quick, about a fifteen-minute treatment. The full effect can take weeks.

One effect was immediate: ileal-colonic radiation enteritis (bowel inflammation). Lots of bowel activity. I'm not going to go into detail, but I was miserable. It began to resolve, but the therapy was not working as I had continuous low back pain, especially by evening—not a good prognosis.

# Chapter 31

The pain continued, and my mobility was becoming impaired. My posture was declining. Another CT scan confirmed my original diagnosis. The third lumbar vertebra is destroyed; only 30 percent remains—total collapse. To make matters worse, my fifth lumbar had slipped, causing lumbar sacral dysfunction.

A neurosurgical consultation told me what I already knew: I needed major spinal stabilization surgery, known as a 360. The first part is an anterior approach with a corpectomy (removing the dead bone) and implanting a stabilizer (looks like a car jack). It's a big operation!

Exposing the L3 is difficult due to the vena cava and large veins, so it's a high-risk surgery. I was ten hours under anesthesia then semi-comatose in the neuro ICU for four days, hallucinating, abdominal distention with compartment syndrome, drug interaction/withdrawal. I thought I was going to die. But I didn't! I was discharged to inpatient rehab and left after only one day to recover at home.

Before you knew it, I was driving and walking without a cane. As a matter of fact, at about the fourth week, I was on stage for our white coat ceremony, where the incoming medical students receive their white coats—a symbolic transition into the profession. I received the Mary E. Luibel Distinguished Service Award from the UNTHSC president. Everyone was amazed at my progress. I believe I am on my way to a much better state. The pathology report showed no residual myeloma, but I caution that it's not gone. My posture is better, and my activity levels are improving. We restarted chemo and will monitor markers.

# Chapter 32

So where do we go from here? An incurable disease but optimism for a few years of good life as we transition to the next phase: giving back. I am grateful to have accumulated a substantial legacy, and Sharon and I have designated endowments to UNTHSC TCOM and the University of Strathclyde. In addition, we established a DO/PhD scholarship to fund two dual-degree students a year. It is a vision of mine to train clinical scientists, for we lack support in this area. We must give back to the institutions that give us the opportunity to succeed.

The Fates continue to weave the fabric of my life. The purest golden thread will always be Sharon. We plan on enjoying each other in the time we have together.

I hope you liked the book, learned some facts, had a few laughs, and sparked your own self-reflection. The title, incidentally, comes from my cardiac training when our chief LBM always had the tech wet his hands while he tied knots; he thought this made the knots more stable. When I started my practice as a cardiothoracic surgeon, I gave the same command.

One final note: A portion of the *Wet My Hands* sales proceeds will go to the general scholarship funds at the Texas College of Osteopathic Medicine in University of North Texas Health Science Center and the University of Strathclyde.

One more thing!

I have been inspired to continue writing about my life's journey, so I have started book 2: "This to Me." So I hope book 1 was entertaining, emotional, and fun. Book 2 will have a different focus.

I will present some of my most interesting patients that I have had the privilege of caring for over the span of my career.

So there's more to come.

Cheers,
Dr. Al Yurvati

# About the Author

Albert H. O-Yurvati, DO, PhD, DFACOS, FICS, FAHA, is a 1986 graduate of the Texas College of Osteopathic Medicine in the University of North Texas Health Science Center. He completed his internship and general surgery residency at Tulsa Regional Medical Center at Tulsa, Oklahoma, and served as chief resident his final year. He then completed a residency in cardiothoracic and vascular surgery at the Deborah Heart and Lung Center in Robert Wood Johnson Medical School at Browns Mills, New Jersey, where he also served as chief resident. He is AOA board certified in cardiothoracic-vascular and general surgery, and he is a fellow of the American College of Surgeons as well as the International College of Surgeons. He was one of the inaugural Distinguished Fellows of the American College of Osteopathic Surgeons.

He completed a PhD in education with a concentration on organizational leadership from Northcentral University. Other educational activities include a graduate certificate from the University of North Texas Toulouse School of Education in teaching and adult learning.

Currently, Dr. O-Yurvati is a tenured DSWOP professor of surgery and chair of the Department of Medical Education at the Texas College of Osteopathic Medicine, and he is a professor of integrative physiology in the Institute of Cardiovascular and Metabolic Disease. He is a visiting professor at the University of Strathclyde in Glasgow, Scotland, in the Department of Biomedical Engineering.

He has received numerous awards from the UNTHSC, including the 2012 Clyde Gallehugh DO Memorial Award and the 2011 President's Award for Clinical Excellence. He also received Doctor of Philanthropy in 2011, and in 2010, he was the recipient of both the

Benjamin L. Cohen Award for Outstanding Research Achievement and the TCOM's Dean's Award for Philanthropy. In addition, he received the Academic Commendation of Excellence (ACE) Award for superior posttenure review.

On a national level, Dr. O-Yurvati was the executive director of the American Osteopathic Board of Surgery. He is actively involved in numerous committees of the ACOS, and he has served as a discipline chair and representative to the board of governors as well as a cardiothoracic educational program director. In 2013, he received the highest award from the American College of Osteopathic Surgeons: the Orel F. Martin Medal. In 2016, he received the ACOS Guy D. Beaumont Education Award.

He is on the editorial board of multiple journals, including the JAOA and *Filtration*. He is a reviewer for many peered journals to include Cardiovascular Research and Experimental Biology and Medicine, Annals of Thoracic Surgery, and the JAOA.

Dr. O-Yurvati has published over one hundred peer-reviewed articles, three book chapters, and numerous abstracts. He is the recipient of over 2.5 million in grants, including NIH, NASA, DOD, and Osteopathic Heritage Foundation funding. He has lectured nationally and internationally. Dr. O-Yurvati is the associate designated institutional official for the Medical City Healthcare Consortium's ACGME-accredited programs. He also served on the ACGME working group for Surgery Milestones 2.0.

Printed in the USA
CPSIA information can be obtained
at www.ICGtesting.com
LVHW021043080424
776753LV00020B/401